ONE THREE NINE INSPIRED

HANNAH'S
DOWN SYNDROME
SUPERPOWERS

BOOK 2

WRITTEN BY LORI LEIGH YARBOROUGH, PT
ILLUSTRATED BY ROKSANA OSLIZLO

Published by One Three Nine Inspired Press
Texas U.S.A.

For permissions, please email:
superkids@onethreenineinspired.com

Library of Congress Control Number: 2019939564
Library of Congress Cataloging-in-Publication Data
Yarborough, Lori

Hannah's Down Syndrome Superpowers/ by Lori Leigh Yarborough; illustrated by Roksana Oslizlo.
Summary: Hannah, superhero princess, explains her Down Syndrome superpowers, how they affect her, and how she's more like other kids than different.

ISBN-13: 978-1-7326381-2-9

Special thanks to Mindy for her helpful input, insightful ideas, and captivating stories about her precious daughter, Hannah.

Disclaimer: This book details the author's personal experiences along with the personal experiences shared by a parent of the child who is featured in the book and their opinions about Down Syndrome. The ideas and suggestions in this book are not intended to diagnose, treat, cure, or prevent any condition. Please consult with your own physician or healthcare provider or specialist regarding the suggestions and recommendations in this book.

To Hannah –
You are wonderfully made,
and a precious, beautiful gift.
-L.L.Y.

Hi. My name is Hannah. And I have **MAGICAL SUPERPOWERS!**

So, I might not actually live in a real castle or have a magic wand, but that doesn't mean I don't have superpowers.

My superpowers come from my . . .

DOWN SYNDROME ABILITIES!

And my Down Syndrome abilities come from an extra chromosome. I know what you're thinking. What in the world are chromosomes? How did I end up with an extra? And why does the number even matter?

Chromosomes are tiny strands that look like threads. They're so small you can only see them with a very powerful microscope. They are in every cell of every living thing. Like me. And you. And my puppy, Pancho.

Chromosomes tell your body how to grow. Most people have 23 pairs. A pair means two. So that makes 46 total. But kids with Down Syndrome have an extra one on the 21st chromosome which gives them 47. This changed the way my brain and body developed.

And **POOF!** I had superpowers.

Did you know most kids with Down Syndrome have certain things in common? Our almond-shaped eyes and somewhat flatter profile make our faces look similar. Some of us even have a single straight line across our palms.

Both boys and girls can have Down Syndrome. But it's not scary. And you can't catch it. Kids with Down Syndrome are just like kids without Down Syndrome.

We're more alike than different

SO LET ME TELL YOU ALL ABOUT MY SUPERPOWERS.

My first superpower is that I'm a . . .

FUN FRIEND

I LOVE fun. And I LOVE friends! If you're playing or having a good time, I want to join in.

PLAYDATES   BIRTHDAY PARTIES

STORY TIME   USING MY IMAGINATION

COLORING   SWINGING   DANCING

DRESSING UP   CARS & TRAINS   DOLLS

PUZZLES   CRAFTS   ART   GAMES

SINGING   BUILDING   LAUGHING

HANGING OUT ON THE PLAYGROUND

HELPFUL HINTS FOR FRIENDS

Your friend with Down Syndrome wants to play and laugh. She wants to be a good friend to you. So be a good friend to her.

Sometimes you might have to show her how to share or take turns. Ask her to join you and your friends. If she can't always keep up, be patient and don't run off and leave her behind.

And, if anyone is unkind or tries to bully your friend, ALWAYS stick up for her.

A fun part of my superpower training is learning . . .

SEVERAL SIMPLE SIGNS

I talk with words AND sign language. The older I get, I use sign language less and words more. Check out some of my first signs.

touch fingers
to mouth
like eating

EAT

bring hand
to mouth
like drinking

DRINK

palms face in
then turn out

ALL DONE

palm helps
the top hand up

HELP

tap fingers
together

MORE

twist wrists
back and forth

PLAY

touch thumb to forehead

DAD

touch thumb to chin

MOM

rub hand in a circle on chest

PLEASE

bring hand out to person you are thanking

THANK YOU

cut out cookie on palm

COOKIE

I LOVE YOU

HELPFUL HINTS FOR FRIENDS

Your friend with Down Syndrome usually understands what you're saying even if it doesn't always seem like it. Talk to him like you talk to your other friends. Sometimes you may need to use fewer words. But for the most part, he likes to listen to your conversation. It helps him feel included.

If your friend is young and has a hard time using words, learn some simple sign language. He'll eventually be able to tell you what he wants. It may take a little longer, but keep smiling, chatting, and playing with him.

Another one of my superpowers is what I like to call the . . .

POWER OF LOVE

Books are written about it. People sing about it. I live it.

My mom says I'm friendly and outgoing to almost everyone.
I love to give people hugs, kisses, and smiles. Even people
I don't know.

Because I'm a cutie, most people hug me right back.

HELPFUL HINTS FOR FRIENDS

Just like you have your own unique and special personality, your friend does too. She
also has the same feelings you do. She can be happy or sad, grouchy or loving, excited
or scared, relaxed or frustrated, and calm or upset. Sometimes she wants to show
affections. Other times she doesn't.

Hugs are nice. But only if someone wants them. Ask first. When your friend hugs YOU,
hug her back. If you're uncomfortable hugging someone you don't know well, it's OKAY
to say you only give hugs to your family and close friends.

My superpower of . . .

TERRIFIC TRUSTER

means I completely trust people all the time. This goes along with my Power of Love. I assume everyone loves me and wants the best for me.

One time there was this guy eating chips at the park, and he held out his bag. How could I resist? Smiling, I walked right over and ate some.

That made my mom frown. She worries I'll trust someone who *doesn't* have my best interests at heart.

HELPFUL HINTS FOR FRIENDS

Your friend with Down Syndrome is probably super friendly. Sometimes this can be a problem. She may not be aware of stranger danger. Help keep her safe by encouraging her not to talk to or hug people she doesn't know. If she looks like she's wandering off from the group, bring her back.

Sometimes my friend, Jacob, feels frustrated by his . . .

SUPER SENSORY CONTROLLER

Every single person has a sensory system. The sensory system is part of how we see, hear, taste, smell, touch, and even move. When it comes to sensory issues, kids with Down Syndrome can be seekers, avoiders, or a little of both.

SEEKERS don't get enough sensory information or are undersensitive to their surroundings.

Sensory Seekers might:
spin and rock
grind their teeth
enjoy bright lights
love to be hugged tightly
chew or lick things

AVOIDERS get too much sensory information or are oversensitive to their surroundings.

Sensory Avoiders might:
decline certain clothes
refuse specific foods
freak out about dirty hands
panic around bright lights
resist wearing shoes

HELPFUL HINTS FOR FRIENDS

New places, people, and situations can be overwhelming. If your friend seems panicked, stay calm and try to figure out what's bothering him. His sensory system might be on overload. Take him someplace quiet where he can get away from bright lights, loud sounds, and crazy chaos.

If your friend is seeking sensory input, help him find safe options by asking his parents what activities would be good for him.

Every great superhero has a team of . . .

SUPER SIDEKICKS

I started walking and talking later than other kids, so my team has been with me since I was little. My three favorite sidekicks are my therapists.

My physical therapist, Robin, helps me with gross motor skills. Those are the big movements I do with my body. We work on balance and muscle strength. We also practice riding a bike and walking up and down stairs.

My occupational therapist, Jill, helps with my fine motor skills. Those are the little movements I do with my hands. We do activities that help me put together puzzles, hold scissors, and write with a pencil. She works on my sensory needs too. That helps me calm myself and stay more focused.

My speech pathologist, Rhonda, helps me with sign language. She uses signs, gestures, and pictures to encourage me to say sounds, words, and short sentences.

Eventually, I'll be able to do most everything other kids can. It just takes my body longer to learn.

My next superpower is . . .

FABULOUS FLEXIBILITY

I can get into all kinds of crazy positions. I really like to
sit with my legs crossed and my feet pulled up where I can see
them.

My body is so loose and relaxed that my mom says sometimes
I look like a wet noodle. Technically, that's called hypotonia.
You say it like this: high-po-tone-ee-ah. It's a big word, but all
it means is that there's a lack of tone in my muscles that makes
me look and feel like a floppy doll.

And that makes everyday things like standing, walking, and
talking take more effort.

A superpower that my friends and family find frustrating is my . . .

STUPENDOUS STUBBORN STREAK

If I don't want it to happen, it's not gonna happen. I can be super-duper stubborn.

Well, most of the time. My mom says with a little coaxing my mind can be changed. Unless I'm scared because I don't understand what's going on and I don't know how to tell you. Or I don't think I can do an activity. Then good luck with that.

HELPFUL HINTS FOR FRIENDS

If your friend is being stubborn, try and figure out WHY. There is almost always a reason. She might not even know the reason. You can give her words or phrases to help her express her feelings.

One way is to remind her why she needs to do something. You can say, "We need to brush your hair so we can go to the store. You wanted to go to the store, right?" Or even, "First, brush your hair. Then, we'll go to the store."

My superpower of . . .

CARING COMPASSION

shows how much I love to be kind. If someone is upset or sad, I'm quick to make the sign for "cry" and give them a big hug and kiss.

When I'm sorry about something, I make the "sorry" sign by balling up my hand up in a fist and rubbing it in a circle on my chest. A lot of times, I'll rub my circle on the person I'm sorry for.

Everyone knows that superpowers come with positives and negatives. Some of the not so great things with Down Syndrome are . . .

MEDICAL MATTERS

Kids with Down Syndrome can have many medical issues. Some kids are healthy but have developmental delays, which means they are behind in skills for their age. Others have more severe issues.

My friend, Caleb, has scars on his chest from surgery for a heart defect he had when he was born. His heart didn't grow or work the way it was supposed to.

Other kids may have stomach troubles that sometimes need surgery to fix, hearing or vision loss, and problems with their lungs.

HELPFUL HINTS FOR FRIENDS

Your friend with Down Syndrome might have to see many kinds of doctors. That can be hard. Be understanding and supportive. Do something nice to show you care.

Because of your friend's extra health issues, he may not have a strong immune system. A normal cold can make your friend a lot sicker than you and take him a lot longer to get well. Even if you're just a little bit sick, stay away until you get better.

My family thinks I'm a . . .

BRILLIANT & BEAUTIFUL BLESSING

My parents weren't sure what to expect when they found out
I was on the way. They had no idea what a treasure I would be.
I'm an important part of my family.

Whatever they're doing, I'm doing right along with them. Going
to the beach. Headed to the lake. Hanging out at the house.
Count me in!

I'm so much like my brothers and other kids my age that sometimes my mom forgets all about my superpowers.

She says I'm sweet, smart, eager to learn, gentle, kind, loving, funny, and the most beautiful gift.

She may have mentioned the words "strong-willed" and "stubborn" too, but it's all good.

YOUR OWN SUPERPOWERS

If you have Down Syndrome, you probably have some of the same superpowers as me and some that are special to you. Write down your name and your Superpowers below.

_____'S SUPERPOWERS

★ _____

★ _____

★ _____

★ _____

★ _____

YOU'RE WONDERFUL!

YOU'RE *amazing* **JUST THE WAY YOU ARE**

YOU'RE VALUABLE!

YOU'RE UNIQUELY YOU

You were put here

for a reason

YOU'RE CRAFTED *with* BEAUTY AND PURPOSE

YOU HAVE SUPERPOWERS!

THERE'S NO ONE *like you!*

My amazing superpowers can bring frustrating challenges. I sometimes have to work hard to get easy, everyday things done. But I'm really just like other kids.

I love my family and friends. I love to have fun. I enjoy movies, games, toys, books, music, using my imagination, and having a good time.

Like you, I have worth, value, purpose, incredible talents, and so much potential. Down Syndrome is only a small part of me.

Every kid needs to know they are wonderfully made. It's important to encourage each other. Let's look for ways to make each other feel special.

Now that I'M feeling encouraged and empowered, my superhero self is going to go dance, laugh, sing, and play princess in my backyard with my puppy.

MEET HANNAH!

Hannah lives in Oklahoma, loves her mom and dad, enjoys dressing up as a princess, playing with her puppy, and hanging out with her friends and brothers.

Each One Three Nine Inspired book is written about a specific child in corroboration with his or her parents. The information given is about that particular child's superpowers but will be relatable to other children with the same diagnosis and abilities.

Hannah's Down Syndrome Superpowers was written with help from Mindy—Hannah's beautiful mom—and told from the perspective of Hannah at age five.

This book is a tool to help children and their friends, family, and caregivers understand kids with Down Syndrome.

All children need to know they're wanted, loved, and special. All children need to know they have superpowers. And all children especially need to know they're wonderfully made.

"I WILL PRAISE YOU BECAUSE I AM
FEARFULLY AND WONDERFULLY MADE;
YOUR WORKS ARE WONDERFUL,
I KNOW THAT FULL WELL."

PSALMS 139:14

The inspirational art on the next page has been designed especially for you. You may cut it out on the lines, pick your favorite side and hang it in an 8 x 10 inch frame.

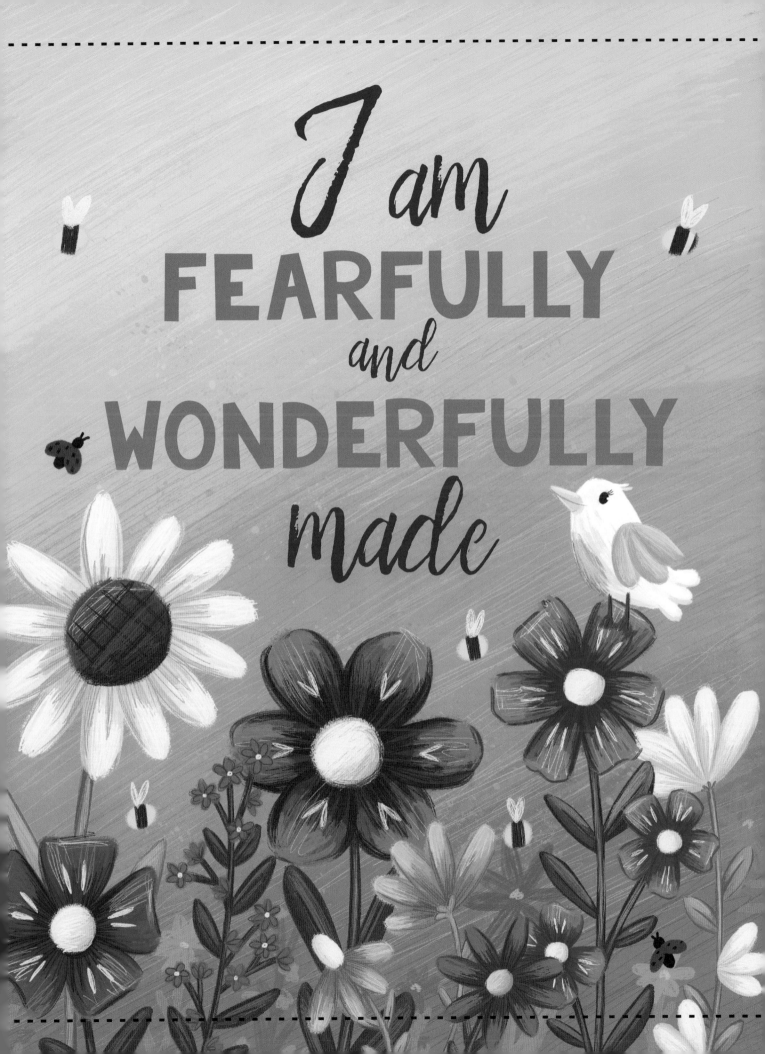

I AM FEARFULLY AND WONDERFULLY MADE

Printed in Poland
by Amazon Fulfillment
Poland Sp. z o.o., Wrocław

24664918R00025